THE 2024 GOOGLE ADS FOR BUSINESS GROWTH AND SUCCESS BLUEPRINT

Unleash the Power of Google Ads to Make Your Business Standout, Get Quality Leads, Maximize Reach, Increase Online and Offline Sales

Sarah Jordan

COPYRIGHT PAGE

Copyright © 2023 by Sarah Jordan.

All rights reserved. No part of this book may be reproduced, distributed, or transmitted in any form or by any means, including photocopying, recording, or other electronic or mechanical methods, without the prior written permission of the publisher, except for brief quotations contained in reviews or other noncommercial uses permitted by copyright law.

The 2024 Google Ads for Business Growth and Success Blueprint is designed to serve as a resource for learning about and getting the most out of Google Ads. Neither is it meant to substitute discussions with trained advertising professionals nor does it represent professional advice.

The author and publisher of this book are not responsible for how the information contained within it is used or abused. It is advised that readers communicate with certified experts or consultants in the field of advertising or marketing to solve specific issues or requirements.

Table of Contents

COPYRIGHT PAGE 2

Table of Contents 4

Chapter 1: Demystifying Google Ads? 1

    Why You Should Use Google Ads for your Marketing Campaign 4

    What Google Ads Offer Your Brand 8

    Understanding How Ads Work 13

Chapter 2: Stepping Into The World of Google Ads 17

    How to Step Up a Google Ads Account 21

    Setting Up an Effective Campaign Structure ... 25

Chapter 3: Keyword Research and Selection 28

Choosing The Right Keywords in Google Ads .. 31

Keyword Research Approaches 34

Benefits of Negative Keywords 38

Chapter 4: Understanding the Different Ad Types and Formats 42

Using the Different Ads Format 46

Using Text Ads 49

Using Display Ads 51

Using Video Ads 53

Using Shopping Ads 58

Chapter 5: How to Segment and Target Your Audience 63

What Audience Targeting Will Get You 67

Benefits of Location Targeting 72

How to Carry Out Audience Segmentation 76

Customize Your Ads to Target Your Audience 78

Chapter 6: Different Approaches to Budgeting and Bidding 83

Fundamentals of Budgeting and Bidding Principles 86

Using Cost-Per-Click (CPC) For Your Ads 91

Chapter 7: Ad Performance and Optimization 96

Understanding A/B Testing and Experimentation 100

Keeping Track of Your Ad's Performance 102

Chapter 8: Different Techniques for Remarketing 106

Setting the Perfect Remarketing Campaign 110

Cost Effective Remarketing Techniques 113

Remarketing Ads for Boosting ROI 117

Chapter 9: Boosting Your Brand Awareness 120

Google Ads and Brand Awareness 121

Compelling Ad Content for Boosting Brand Recognition 124

Target Audiences Reach and Engagement 127

Chapter 10: SEO and Google Ads 132

Boosting Ad Performance with SEO 134

Ads Optimization for Increased Search Engine Visibility 136

Chapter 11: Instant Results and Boosting Visibility 139

Techniques that Generates Instant Results 141

Approaches to Boost Visibility Using Click-Through Rates 145

Google Ads that Drives Instant Conversions .. 150

Performance Assessment for Timely Results .. 153

Chapter 1: Demystifying Google Ads?

Previously known as Google AdWords, Google Ads is now Google's principal online advertising platform. It is currently the largest advertising network in the World Wide Web.

Google Ads is a pay-per-click (PPC) advertising service that places commercial content directly inside Google's search engine results. Bidding on certain keywords allows businesses to have their ads displayed at the top of search results, with costs incurred only when a user clicks on the ad.

Ad placement is more targeted since this platform makes use of Google's vast data pool and sophisticated targeting options. Google Ads allows you to reach a wide variety of online audiences by capitalizing on Google's position as the most popular search engine in the world.

Advertisements are displayed not just on Google's search results page but also extend to platforms such as Google Maps, Google Shopping, and different partner sites exhibiting text advertisements.

Google Ads is structured as an auction marketplace, where advertisers may bid on ad impressions and clicks. Ads presented are prioritized based on quality scores to provide a positive user experience.

Google Ads might be intimidating to company owners because of all the possibilities and risks involved. Mismanagement of advertising campaigns might result in significant financial loss, but if used properly, this advertising instrument could completely transform a company.

It is essential, however, to have a firm grasp on the platform's fundamental workings. This review attempts to illustrate the functions and benefits of Google Ads, highlighting its relevance in contacting and engaging potential customers actively searching products or services, hence improving business exposure and growth.

Why You Should Use Google Ads for your Marketing Campaign

There are several compelling reasons why organizations should use Google Ads for marketing. Since Google is the most popular search engine, the platform guarantees exposure to a huge audience by placing advertising in relevant search results, on partner websites, on YouTube, and more.

Google Ads' strength is the specificity and efficiency with which it reaches its target audience. Advertisers may utilize specialized targeting choices based on demographics, interests, behaviors, and keywords, ensuring ads are viewed by individuals actively seeking products or services.

Google Ads also offers adjustable spending limits to suit different marketing budgets. Advertisers, no matter how big or little, are given the freedom to set and change their own expenditure limits.

The site is based on a pay-per-click (PPC) business model, which means that advertisers only have to fork out cash when people actually click on their adverts. Payment is dependent on user activity, making this a measurable and efficient kind of advertising that is also cost-effective.

Google Ads also offers in-depth stats and insights, allowing marketers to monitor campaign success in near real-time. Using this function, campaign managers may make educated choices and fine-tune their strategies based on hard facts.

Ads may be made, released, and shown in Google search results lightning fast thanks to Google Ads' streamlined workflow and flexible settings. Agility in campaign management is provided by giving advertisers full authority over ad creation, spending, and deployment.

Text advertising, visually appealing display ads, and even videos are just some of the ad kinds that may be found on this platform. Because of this variety, advertisements may be crafted with more specificity.

Google Ads boosts brand awareness and market penetration by placing advertisements in relevant search results and across other websites.

Strategic bidding and optimization give marketers a leg up on the competition, allowing them to beat rivals and get a larger proportion of the market.

Google Ads continuously provides new features and tools, allowing businesses options to exploit the newest innovations in digital advertising, making it a crucial and high-impact tool in today's digital marketing scene.

What Google Ads Offer Your Brand

There are a lot of positives that come along with using Google Ads for advertising purposes. The platform's presence in SERPs, on partner sites, on YouTube, and across other online mediums guarantees extensive exposure to a large audience.

Additionally, Google Ads allows marketers to target certain demographics, interests, behaviors, and geographies with pinpoint accuracy. Ads are more likely to be viewed by those who are actively interested in them because to this pinpoint targeting.

Companies can choose their own budgets and modify them as necessary. The platform can work with a wide range of budgets, from the very little to the very large.

Because it is based on a pay-per-click (PPC) model, Google advertisements guarantees payment based on real interaction, as marketers only pay when consumers click on their advertisements.

The platform gives in-depth measurements and insights. Marketers can see how well their efforts are doing in real time, allowing them to make educated decisions based on data and making quick modifications to optimize results.

Advertisers can easily have their advertisements up and running and visible in search results using Google advertisements. They may be as flexible as needed in managing their campaigns since they have complete say over the ads' content, spending, and timing.

Google advertisements allows for flexible and specialized advertising campaigns by offering a wide variety of ad types, from plain text advertisements to visually appealing display and video ads.

By being prominently shown on search results and across partner websites, Google Ads greatly enhances brand visibility and exposure to potential customers.

Successfully outperforming competitors and increasing market share may be attained by firms through strategic bidding, optimization, and appropriate targeting.

In addition, Google Ads is constantly updating with new features and capabilities, giving companies the chance to take advantage of cutting-edge digital advertising methods and remain competitive in the ever-shifting field of online marketing.

Google Ads has several benefits, such as widespread exposure and pinpoint targeting, adjustable spending limits, and a pay-per-click strategy that guarantees efficiency and quantifiable outcomes. It's a potent tool that gives organizations the nimbleness, command, and constant innovation they need to grow their online presence and boost conversions.

Understanding How Ads Work

In order for marketers to reach their intended audience, Google Ads employs a multi-step procedure. Advisors pick appropriate terms to describe their offerings. Ads connected to these keywords may appear when consumers conduct similar searches on Google.

Auctions play a crucial role in this procedure. Google holds an auction to decide which advertisements will be shown in response to a user's search query. The advertiser's price, ad quality, and the anticipated impact of ad extensions are only few of the criteria taken into account in this auction.

Ad Rank, a statistic that takes into account bid, quality score, and ad extensions, is used to order ads. Typically, the ad with the highest Ad Rank is shown first.

Text advertising, image advertisements, video ads, and more are just some of the ad types available with Google advertising. These advertisements may display in the Google Search results, on Display Network sites that are partners, on YouTube, or on other Google-owned or -operated sites and services.

When an auction is triggered by a user's search query, the outcome is determined by Google's algorithms. Successful adverts are presented to the user, and if a user clicks on the ad, the advertiser pays a cost per click (CPC).

Marketers decide on a spending cap and select demographic, geographic, interest, and device targeting choices. With these options, you can control who sees your adverts and where they appear.

With Google advertising, marketers can monitor the efficacy of their advertising in real time thanks to a wealth of data and insights provided by the platform. Based on these information, advertisers may fine-tune their ads in real time.

Ads on Google are displayed to users based on their search queries and are obtained through an auction system where marketers bid on keywords. Advertisers may target particular audiences using the platform's flexible ad formats, placements, and targeting choices. Advertisers may maximize the success and efficiency of their campaigns by constant tracking and tweaking.

Chapter 2: Stepping Into The World of Google Ads

Incorporating Google Ads into a company's online advertising strategy might be a thrilling new undertaking. The first step is to create a Google Ads account by entering your email address, company website, and preferred currency type.

Establish whether or whether you want to advertise primarily to improve website traffic, sales, brand recognition, or leads. Choose a campaign format that corresponds to your intended outcome.

Determine who you want to see your ads by picking a set of characteristics (demographic, geographic, interest, or behavior) that best represent your ideal consumer.

Do some digging to find the best keywords to use in connection with your company. Use Google's Keyword Planner to research relevant and successful keywords.

Construct enticing ad copy by writing concisely and interestingly, and include appropriate images or videos if they would complement your ad.

Determine how much money you're prepared to spend and what kind of bidding method you want to use, such as manual CPC or automated bidding.

Consider using ad extensions to boost the exposure and interaction of your advertising by adding more information like call buttons, site links, or geographical details.

Ensure that your advertising link consumers to relevant and optimized landing pages on your website. These pages should complement the ads' content and provide a consistent flow for the reader.

Once your campaign is online, be sure to keep an eye on critical metrics like click-through rates, conversions, and expenses on a consistent basis. You may use this information to fine-tune your marketing.

Google Ads is always evolving, so it's important to keep up with the latest features, modifications, and best practices. Learn more by attending webinars, perusing Google's official resources, and looking into other educational options.

Strategic planning, ongoing learning, and incremental improvements are all part of the process of getting started with Google Ads. By following these early steps and keeping proactive in maintaining and optimizing your campaigns, you can create a strong foundation for effective online advertising using Google Ads.

How to Step Up a Google Ads Account

There are a few essential actions to take when setting up your Google Ads account, which will provide the groundwork for all of your future advertising efforts. Get started with Google Ads by creating an account with your existing Google details. Specify your company's essentials like a website, email address, and preferred currency.

Verify your account's basic information, such as your contact info, billing info, and administrative settings, by clicking through the account setup wizard. The Campaigns tab is where you should go to build your first campaign. Based on your marketing objectives, select a relevant campaign type like Search, Display, Shopping, Video, or App.

Specify the name of your campaign, your bidding method, your budget, your preferred locations, the beginning and ending dates of your campaign, the language you wish to use, and other pertinent variables. Make sub-campaigns within the overall one, each devoted to a certain set of topics or items. Assign keywords, advertisements, and landing pages to ad groups to maintain consistency and relevancy.

Find and choose keywords that accurately describe the services you provide. Choose keywords that correctly match what your clients are searching for to enhance ad relevancy. Create engaging ad copy that works with your chosen ad medium. Make sure it's relevant to your chosen keywords and the information shown on your landing page.

Use ad extensions to give your adverts a boost. Enhance the ad experience and offer value for users by including additional information like call buttons, site links, geographical facts, and structured snippets. Conversion monitoring allows you to see what happens to users when they click on your adverts. This data helps analyze campaign success and supports in improving plans for improved performance.

It's important to double-check the campaign's settings, advertisements, and targeting methods before releasing it into the wild. When everything has been double-checked, you may launch the campaign and begin reaching your demographic with your advertising. It is important to pay close attention to the finer points while setting up your Google advertising account, aligning your keywords, advertising, and targeting, and constantly monitoring your account's success metrics. If you follow these instructions to the letter, you'll have a Google Ads account that's set up for success.

Setting Up an Effective Campaign Structure

Effective advertising relies heavily on Google Ads' campaign structure. At their most basic level, advertising campaigns incorporate individual advertising objectives like the promotion of certain items, the generation of website traffic, or the raising of brand awareness.

To further refine and organize your advertisements, you may create ad groups under each campaign. Ads are organized into groups based on topics or items to better target particular audiences with relevant content.

Ads are displayed in response to user queries that include selected keywords that are part of an ad group. Advertisements are created for these categories, coordinating with chosen keywords and directing visitors to the most pertinent sections of your website. Ad extensions provide more data or functionality, increasing your advertising' visibility and effectiveness.

Campaign budgets determine the total amount to be spent on a given campaign, whereas keyword bidding establishes the maximum price an advertiser is prepared to pay for a certain activity.

Ads may be more structured and targeted if their hierarchical placement is known, improving relevance, alignment with corporate goals, and audience reach. Advertisers may improve the efficacy and return on investment of their campaigns by tweaking each component individually.

Chapter 3: Keyword Research and Selection

Effective Google Ads campaigns are built on the foundation of thorough keyword research and selection. Understanding your company, its products, and your target market is the first step.

Create a list of seed keywords by thinking about the most basic terms that describe your offerings. This first list will provide the basis for more investigation.

To find more keywords, use a keyword research tool like SEMrush, Ahrefs, Ubersuggest, or the Google Keyword Planner. You may refine and expand your keyword pool with the help of these tools, which offer insights about search traffic, competitiveness, and related keyword ideas.

Think on how useful and specific each keyword is. Use keywords that people are likely to type into a search engine to find what you're selling. You could think about using long-tail keywords, which are more specialized terms. These usually have less competitors and more enthusiastic buyers.

Incorporate "negative" keywords into your approach to filter out unwanted results. Refine your targeting and boost your advertisements' efficacy by using negative keywords like "cheap" or "free" that aren't relevant to your business.

Group the selected keywords into topics or groups, ensuring harmony with the ad text and landing sites. Maintaining relevance and consistency across ads is easier when keywords are organized into structured ad groups.

Your choice of keywords should be monitored and improved on a regular basis in light of relevant metrics and hard facts. As a result of this iterative process, your campaigns will always be optimized for the most relevant and successful keywords.

Ads that are relevant to their target demographic and that attract high-quality visitors will perform better in Google Ads, and your campaign as a whole will benefit from careful keyword research and selection.

Choosing The Right Keywords in Google Ads

Successful internet advertising strategies are built on carefully selected keywords for use in Google Ads. These terms play a crucial role in connecting people's queries with the advertisements that firms show. Customers' most likely search terms for a certain product/service/information are then matched with carefully selected keywords.

The relevance of adverts to a user's search is mostly dependent on the use of appropriate keywords. When a person searches for a term or phrase that matches the specified keywords in a campaign, the ad can be displayed. Therefore, it is essential to have a thorough comprehension of keywords in order to maximize the reach and relevancy of advertisements.

The procedure is picking a set of keywords that work well together and are highly relevant to what a business has to offer and what people are looking for. These keywords are categorized into ad categories that promote similar goods or services. Ad relevancy and the chance of reaching the proper audience may be increased by crafting attractive ad text and employing these chosen keywords.

Advertisers may improve and broaden their keyword selection with the use of keyword research tools, which aid in the discovery of new terms, analysis of search traffic, and comprehension of user behavior. Negative keywords are another important consideration since they help filter out non-relevant search results.

Keywords are the link between user intent and ad exposure. Businesses may improve the effectiveness of their advertisements by choosing, grouping, and optimizing keywords to increase their relevance to the target audience. Successful Google Ads campaigns rely on the knowledge and use of keywords.

Keyword Research Approaches

Tools and tactics for doing keyword research are of paramount importance for developing profitable Google Ads campaigns.

Keyword Analysis Software

There are a number of helpful resources for conducting keyword research, including:

The free Google Keyword Planner may help you find new phrases, research search traffic, and estimate the level of competition for certain terms. Both SEMrush and Ahrefs are great for researching keywords and analyzing the competition.

While Ahrefs provides keyword difficulty scores, SEMrush can help you find keywords used by your competitors and see holes in your own approach. As a free resource, Ubersuggest is helpful for novices since it offers keyword suggestions, search traffic data, and keyword difficulty measures. Moz's Keyword Explorer provides extensive keyword data, such as difficulty ratings and suggested priorities.

Techniques for Researching Keywords

There are a number of ways to improve your keyword research:

Seed keywords are the first terms you should study, and they should be closely relevant to your company. Perform a competition study with the help of a tool like SEMrush or Ahrefs to learn about the keywords they are utilizing.

Use long-tail keywords, which are more specialized terms with lower competition and the potential to attract highly engaged clients. Keywords should be chosen with the user's information, product, or service-seeking purpose in mind.

Keywords that change with the seasons might help firms that sell perishable goods or services adapt their marketing to seasonal demand. To attract clients in a certain region, you should use keywords from that region.

Ad optimization and traffic reduction can be achieved through the use of negative keywords. Always keep your keyword list up-to-date depending on results and user behavior changes.

Ad relevancy may be improved by organizing keywords into thematic or product-based ad groups with proper naming conventions. Ad placement precision may be adjusted using several match kinds, including wide match, phrase match, and exact match.

By combining these methods with keyword research tools, you can be confident that your Google Ads campaigns will reach the correct people, become more relevant to them, and ultimately provide better results. Online advertising can only be sustainable if it is constantly optimized and adjusted in response to new data and emerging trends.

Benefits of Negative Keywords

When using Google Ads, it is essential to include negative keywords. They act as filters, protecting advertisers from having their adverts displayed in response to queries that have nothing to do with their products or services. Several crucial factors contribute to their significance:

To better target your advertisements, you may use negative keywords to filter out queries that aren't relevant to your business. Using "cheap" and "free" as negative keywords may prohibit your ad from showing up for visitors searching for low-cost or free products, for instance, if you offer high-end products.

Negative keywords save money since they filter out non-essential queries and reduce wasteful clicks. This enhances the overall efficiency of your ad spend, ensuring that your cash is utilized on more quality leads, thus decreasing expenses per click and boosting return on investment.

Ads containing negative keywords have a better chance of being seen to users who are interested in what you have to offer. This enhances the relevancy of your adverts, leading to more meaningful interactions and perhaps greater conversion rates.

Increased CTR A targeted and specific audience is more likely to click on your ads. By excluding irrelevant search terms from your ad's targeting, negative keywords improve clickthrough rates.

You may improve your ad rank by using negative keywords effectively, which will increase the relevancy and clickthrough rate (CTR) of your ads. This, in turn, can improve rankings in search results and reduce the price of premium ad spots.

Simply said, using negative keywords in your Google advertisements strategy will help your advertisements reach the target demographic more efficiently, which will boost your campaign's overall performance while cutting down on wasteful spending. Maintaining a campaign's efficacy and relevance over time requires routinely analyzing and updating negative keyword lists.

Chapter 4: Understanding the Different Ad Types and Formats

Google Ads offers a wide variety of ad layouts and sizes to suit a wide range of marketing objectives and mediums.

Text-based search advertising are displayed on Google's search engine results pages in response to users entering relevant search terms. They are made up of titles, synopses, and URLs and are aimed at those who have entered relevant search phrases.

In contrast, display adverts are shown in a visual format across a collection of partner websites and typically make use of pictures, rich media, or videos. They are directed at certain people, groups, or subjects in an effort to raise awareness for a brand or to sell a specific product.

Bumper advertising and video discovery ads are two types of video advertisements that may or may not be skipped when they show before, during, or after a video on YouTube. They are useful for engaging information, storytelling, and presenting items or services.

Google's shopping advertisements feature photos, prices, and the names of participating retailers right above the search results. These take advantage of the Merchant Center account's product data, making them perfect for stores.

App adverts are meant to promote mobile apps, promoting downloads or increasing user engagement. The Google Display Network now supports responsive advertisements, which automatically resize themselves to fill any available ad space.

Mobile-optimized call-only adverts appear in search engine results and prompt consumers to dial a phone number instead of clicking through to a company's website. advertisements with location extensions, call buttons, and instructions to a store's physical location are all examples of local advertisements.

Google Discover feed, Gmail tabs, and the YouTube home feed all have visually appealing discovery advertising. Their goal is to maximize their exposure to users across all of these channels.

Your advertising goals, intended demographic, and preferred medium should all be considered before settling on an ad structure and style. If you want your advertising efforts to generate the most interest and sales, you must adapt your ad copy to each individual format and medium.

Using the Different Ads Format

Ad sizes and shapes in Google Ads may be customized to meet a broad range of situations and channels for advertising. Google's search results pages feature text-based search advertisements that are triggered by a user's query. These results are tailored to users who have entered specific search terms and consist of titles, summaries, and URLs.

In contrast, display advertising are exhibited in a visual style across a range of partner websites and often make use of photographs, rich media, or videos. They are aimed at specific audiences with the goal of promoting a product or increasing its sales.

There are two sorts of video advertisements that can appear before, during, or after a video on YouTube: bumper ads and video discovery ads. They are great for telling stories, showcasing products, and sharing information.

Above the search results, Google displays shopping ads that include images, prices, and names of participating stores. These are great for shops since they draw on the product information stored in your Merchant Center account.

The goal of app marketing is to increase mobile app installs and/or user participation. Ads that adapt their size to the available real estate on the Google Display Network can now be shown.

Ads tailored for mobile devices that merely provide a phone number to call rather than a website link are becoming increasingly common. Examples of local ads are those that provide a location extension, a phone number to contact, or explicit directions to the store's actual location.

Eye-catching discovery ads may be seen across several Google products, including the Discover feed, Gmail tabs, and the YouTube home feed. They want as many people as possible to see their content across all of these platforms.

You should think about your advertising objectives, target audience, and media of choice before deciding on ad structure and design. To maximize the impact of your marketing campaigns and their resulting sales, you must customize the text of your ads for each platform.

Using Text Ads

There are a number of tried-and-true methods for writing effective text adverts. Create a compelling title that is both eye-catching and pertinent to the user's search query by emphasizing your product's unique selling qualities or current promotions.

Use the lines after the headline to provide more detail on the advantages or solutions you're offering, and be sure to end with a compelling call to action. You can increase the likelihood that your ad will be shown in response to relevant search queries by clearly communicating your unique value proposition and highlighting the features, benefits, or offers that are most appealing to your target audience, and by using relevant keywords within the ad copy.

A compelling call to action, such as "Shop Now," "Learn More," or "Sign Up Today," encourages consumers to interact with your ad by providing a distinct next step. Be detailed and genuine, and put the emphasis on the advantages your product or service provides rather than the characteristics it offers.

Make sure the information in your ads is true and not overstated, and that it relates to the page readers would reach if they click on your ad. Finally, you may improve your ad's exposure and reach by adding ad extensions like as site links, callouts, and structured snippets. Text advertisements that effectively engage their audience and deliver greater results may be created by adhering to these best practices and regularly testing and tweaking ad versions.

Using Display Ads

Display ad graphic design requires a careful mix of artistic skill and commercial savvy. Selecting eye-catching images, keeping brand consistency, and providing a clear, short message that compliments the visual aspects are crucial in producing effective display advertisements. In addition, guiding user engagement and promoting instant action by including a pertinent and conspicuous call to action (CTA). Assuring a uniform and visually attractive experience across platforms, responsive design adapts to the dimensions of the viewing device.

It's crucial to create a streamlined design that emphasizes the product's benefits while also catering to the target market's requirements. Conducting A/B testing, reviewing performance metrics, and following to ad regulations are essential elements in refining and optimizing ad design for improved engagement and conversions. An effective layout guarantees a smooth flow of information and directs the audience's attention by strategically placing visual and textual components in a clear hierarchy.

Display advertising that appeal with the audience and encourage desired actions are created when powerful graphics are combined with strategic design considerations, brand consistency, compelling text, and user-focused interaction. Display advertising may be a strong tool for brand promotion and engagement, but only if it is professionally designed and performed visually.

Using Video Ads

Video commercials are an effective method of attracting and holding viewers' attention. There are a few critical processes and factors to think about while creating effective video advertisements. Start with a clear statement of the advertisement's purpose, such as "to increase brand awareness," "to increase conversions," "to promote a product," and so on. The creative process can be directed by a well-defined objective.

Every video advertisement relies heavily on its script. Create a clear, convincing narrative that communicates your message effectively to your intended audience. The screenplay should be interesting to read, easy to understand, and convey a powerful message that matches the ideals of your brand or the advantages of your providing.

The graphics should be planned once the writing is complete. Creating a storyboard for your video might help you plan out its structure and make sure you don't forget any key sections. Colors, visuals, and sceneries should all work in tandem with the screenplay to create the intended effect on the viewer.

Choose tunes or effects that complement the video and help establish the mood you want to convey. Mood-setting music has a powerful effect on how people respond to your message. Consider royalty-free or licensed music that resonates with your business and the ad's subject.

Filming, editing, and creating the video are all part of the real creation process. The video's production value can be increased by using high-end camera gear and editing tools. Pay close attention to the quality of the film and the editing if you want a professional result.

After the video has been made, it is crucial to test it extensively and tweak it for the best results. In order to improve the ad, testing entails keeping an eye on interaction rates and collecting user feedback. What works best with the target audience may be determined through A/B testing of several iterations.

Make sure your video ad satisfies the technical needs of the platform it will be presented on by adhering to the platform's standards and specifications. Depending on the advertising platform, this may include adhering to strict guidelines regarding video duration, aspect ratio, and file type.

Successful video advertisements are the result of meticulous preparation, innovative thinking, and an intimate familiarity with the intended viewers. Businesses may develop effective video commercials that engage with their viewers and accomplish the required marketing objectives by adopting a disciplined strategy and improving the video based on performance data.

Using Shopping Ads

Shopping Ads are an integral part of cutting-edge digital marketing strategies since they epitomize a data-driven method of promoting and selling products online. These advertisements reflect a technological worldview in both their approach and execution since they were designed specifically for online shopping.

Utilizing Product Information

To be effective, Shopping Ads require detailed product information, which may be provided via a merchant's feed in Google Merchant Center. Information like photographs, pricing, and shop locations may be shown immediately in search results with the help of this data. By using this technological infrastructure, businesses are better able to reach their target audience and deliver relevant products to shoppers.

Exposing Products in a Live Environment

These advertisements use cutting-edge technological methods to dynamically showcase items across a variety of Google services. Not only do they show up in Google's search results, but also on the Google Display Network, where they might be seen by those who are considering making a purchase. These ads are more likely to result in a conversion since they are tailored to the individual user and their search query.

Intelligent Campaign Optimization

Shopping Ads-based e-commerce marketing campaigns are dependent on technology-driven optimization strategies. Machine learning algorithms, automated bidding techniques, and dynamic retargeting work together to maximize the campaign's exposure, interaction, and outcome. These technical aids modify the campaign in response to user actions and market tendencies, boosting efficiency.

Visual Appeal and Usability

Visual components are heavily used in shopping ads to create a more interesting and user-friendly environment for consumers. An appealing user interface, along with eye-catching product photos and comprehensive product details, is crucial to attracting and retaining customers. The user experience is improved as a result of the emphasis on high-quality images and product information.

E-commerce campaigns that make use of Shopping Ads need to evolve and adapt in light of new technologies and changes in customer behavior. Constant tweaking and optimization of these efforts for optimum effect and sales necessitates keeping abreast of new features, trends, and algorithms.

E-commerce campaigns that make use of Shopping Ads show a comprehensive approach to product marketing by merging technology and data-driven approaches, providing customers with an entertaining and efficient way to browse and purchase products.

Chapter 5: How to Segment and Target Your Audience

Google Ads, like most digital advertising platforms, allows advertisers to target specific audiences based on demographic and interest data. The gist is as follows:

Audiences may be targeted based on their age, gender, income, education, marital status, and other characteristics using demographic targeting. Ads that are targeted to certain demographics are more likely to resonate with those people.

Advertisers can target certain nations, regions, cities, or even a set distance surrounding a given location using a technique called "geographic targeting." It's perfect for companies aiming for either domestic or international clientele.

Users' search histories, browsing patterns, interests, and intent signals may all be used to create a detailed profile of an individual, which is what behavioral targeting is all about. By analyzing user actions, advertisers may better target their messages.

Advertisements may now be tailored to the interests of individual users. Information about a customer's tastes may be used to send them offers for related goods and services.

Users who have already interacted with a website or mobile app are the focus of remarketing efforts. Targeted advertisements are displayed to consumers who have demonstrated interest but have not yet taken the required action.

Ads are contextually targeted when they are presented in relevant surroundings, such as on certain web pages depending on the content or keywords of the page.

advertising may be adjusted for the user's device of choice through a process called "device targeting," in which advertising are created specifically for desktop computers, mobile phones, or tablets.

Custom intent audiences are produced based on consumers' search activity on Google properties. People that are looking into a product or service can be reached more easily this way.

By reaching out to people who are similar to, or "look like," an existing customer base or predetermined group, lookalike audiences help campaigns reach more people.

Advertisers may narrow their emphasis by using these targeting and segmentation approaches to reach just the people most likely to interact with their content. Ads that are tailored to a certain audience not only have a higher probability of being effective, but also a higher return on investment.

What Audience Targeting Will Get You

There is a wide variety of audience targeting options available in digital advertising, allowing marketers to zero in on certain subsets of the population based on demographics, interests, and more.

To ensure that advertising initiatives reach the intended demographic, familiarity with these variables is essential. Key audience targeting possibilities are outlined below.

Age, gender, income, education level, and marital status are just few examples of the demographics that can be used for this type of targeting. Advertisers can target specific demographics based on how well they fit with their goods.

Targeting people based on what they want to do for fun is called "interest-based targeting." It tracks people as they navigate the web so that you can find out what they're interested in and market to them.

Targeting consumers based on their prior behaviors, preferences, and interactions with other users online is called behavioral targeting. It makes use of information about where you go and what you do online.

Remarketing (or retargeting) is a technique used to reach out to people who have visited or used a website or mobile app before but have not yet converted. It offers adverts to these visitors when they surf other websites or platforms.

Ads on a website are contextually relevant if they are relevant to the page the user is now viewing. Ads that are contextually relevant to the user's current activity are displayed.

Targeting based on a user's nation, city, zip code, or distance from a certain area is known as "geographic" or "location-based" targeting. In particular, it helps local companies target people in their immediate vicinity.

Users can be targeted differently depending on the type of device they are using (desktop, mobile, or tablet) via device targeting. It aids in enhancing the quality of the advertising experience for the end customer.

Custom and Lookalike Audiences: Custom audiences are produced using existing customer data, allowing targeting specific lists or consumer groups. Lookalike audiences are newly identified audiences that are similar to existing clients.

Advertisers may design more targeted and effective campaigns if they have a firm grasp of and make good use of these audience targeting choices. Each choice provides a unique channel for reaching out to different subsets of the overall audience, paving the door for more targeted and relevant advertising. Successful use of these targeting choices allows firms to considerably increase the effectiveness and return on investment of their advertising initiatives.

Benefits of Location Targeting

Advertisers using digital advertising platforms like Google Ads can employ a feature called "location targeting" to narrow the geographic scope of their campaigns' reach. The relevance and fundamental features of location targeting are as follows.

Targeting a specific geographic area is a great strategy for firms that focus on a small geographical area or niche market. It makes adverts more relevant to consumers in the specified area by ensuring sure they are viewed by people who are really located there.

Advertisers may reach their target demographic more successfully by adapting their campaigns to specific geographic regions by include language, cultural, or geographical references that are relevant to the target market. Engagement and conversion rates both benefit from this type of individualization.

Reduced waste of advertising dollars on people outside of a company's service region is one major benefit of geotargeting. Spending on advertisements is maximized since they are shown to those who are most likely to be interested in them.

Ads can be displayed prominently to visitors seeking for comparable items or services within a certain region, giving local companies an advantage over their competitors.

Advertisements might highlight location-specific deals, promotions, or events, drawing in clients who are more likely to take advantage of them since they are closer to where they live.

Users on the go may be reached by brick-and-mortar companies thanks to mobile location targeting. Targeting potential clients based on their location is made possible by mobile devices.

Location targeting helps multinational firms strike a good mix between global reach and local relevance. It helps tailor the marketing strategy so that it is more relevant to a wide range of local audiences.

Insights & Performance Monitoring: By tracking how ads work in various markets, businesses may learn how successful their campaigns are in various areas, providing data for more precise targeting in the future.

Ads that take use of location targeting can more accurately reach their intended demographic. It's a smarter, more targeted way to reach potential consumers in certain areas, so you can get the most out of your marketing budget.

How to Carry Out Audience Segmentation

To divide a large target market into more precise groups based on features or attributes, advertising relies heavily on demographic and audience segmentation tactics.

Age, gender, income, education, employment, marital status, and family size are just some of the observable factors that may be used for audience segmentation. Using this technique, one may learn about the core characteristics and habits of a certain customer demographic. Using demographic segmentation, a business may create a product aimed squarely at the young professional market, taking into account the group's disposable income and preferred way of life.

In contrast, audience segmentation explores not just a group's demographic characteristics, but also its psychographic, behavioral, and attitude traits. It looks at things like who people are as individuals and what they're into or what they buy. The method's ultimate goal is to compile in-depth client profiles, which will in turn provide more targeted and efficient advertising campaigns. A tech firm, for instance, may divide its customers into subsets based on factors such as their level of technological sophistication, their enthusiasm for particular types of technology, and their loyalty to particular product lines and features.

Marketers may better target their efforts by segmenting their audiences based on demographics or a more refined audience study. It provides individualized message and targeted offers, ensuring that the marketing efforts resonate better with the intended demographic. Understanding the various subsets of a company's client base allows for better targeted marketing efforts that strike a more personal chord with consumers.

Customize Your Ads to Target Your Audience

Customizing ad distribution for target audiences entails a complete method to adjust how and when ads are presented to certain user segments efficiently. The first step is to divide your intended audience into distinct subgroups defined by shared characteristics such as demographics, interests, habits, or previous encounters. Make use of your ad platform's audience data and analytics to divide your target audience into subsets and provide them ads that are more relevant to them.

The next step in finding the best hours and days to show your adverts is ad scheduling. Ads should be scheduled to appear at peak user activity periods for optimum visibility, and this decision should be made based on when your target audience is most engaged and likely to engage.

Ad distribution may be tailored to specific regions with the use of geographic targeting, making sure that your adverts only appear to consumers in those areas where they would be most effective. This involves zeroing down on certain towns, regions, or even nations where your target audience resides via geotargeting techniques.

Tailoring ad distribution based on the devices your target utilizes is another major factor. Ads should be formatted and designed differently for mobile, desktop, and tablet platforms to provide the best possible user experience.

Controlling ad frequency avoids consumers from being inundated with the same ad again, and ad rotation settings allow for even presentation of multiple ad types to your audience.

By using remarketing, you can reach out to people who have shown interest in your business before and clicked on one of your adverts. In addition, do not waste money advertising to people who have already converted.

It might be helpful to modify ad distribution in response to seasonal patterns or significant events in a certain sector. Holidays, sales seasons, and other occasions relevant to your business should each have their own dedicated campaign.

Advertising that takes into account the linguistic preferences of its intended audience can more successfully reach a wide variety of people.

Lastly, ongoing A/B testing, optimization, and analysis of performance indicators assist refine and optimize ad distribution techniques based on each audience segment's success. Marketers may improve audience engagement and boost conversions by targeting certain demographics and psychographics and then adjusting based on data-driven insights.

Chapter 6: Different Approaches to Budgeting and Bidding

Ad management tools like Google Ads necessitate careful planning of advertising budgets and bidding methods. These components play a significant part in ensuring that your adverts are properly presented to the correct audience at the right time while retaining control over spending.

The importance of a well-thought-out budget cannot be overstated. Considerations such as advertising goals, keyword competitiveness, and overarching marketing strategy will inform the daily or monthly budget you choose for your campaign. Having a set spending limit prevents you from going overboard, while also giving you room to maneuver dependent on how well your campaign does.

There are a variety of bidding strategies that may be implemented to achieve a variety of campaign goals. Manual bidding allows bids to be established at will, providing full command but necessitating constant oversight.

To achieve predetermined objectives, such as increasing clicks or sales, automated bidding makes automated bid modifications using machine learning. Enhanced CPC combines manual bidding with automated bid modifications for more probable conversion clicks. Bids can be optimized based on past data utilizing target CPA or ROAS methods, which zero down on specific expenses or intended returns. Bids are automatically adjusted by tactics designed to maximize clicks or conversions while staying within a certain budget.

Ads that reach their target demographic while keeping expenses in check are the result of careful budgeting and strategic bidding. Improving ad performance and increasing return on investment requires constant monitoring and modifications depending on campaign success and corporate goals.

Fundamentals of Budgeting and Bidding Principles

Google Ads campaign optimization relies heavily on careful planning of spending and bidding. The following is an explanation of these fundamental points:

Budget Allocation and Daily Spending Limits: How much money can you afford to spend each day on advertising? Create a marketing plan and spending plan that complement each other and your overall business objectives.

Establish a maximum CPC bid, or the most money you're prepared to spend per click on your ad, as part of your cost-per-click (CPC) strategy. Your ad's visibility and placement on the site are both affected by the amount you're willing to offer.

Budgeting for Campaigns: Distribute funds among various campaigns in accordance with their relative importance, past successes, and future aims. Spending for any campaign should reflect its intended outcomes.

Regularly evaluate the results of your campaigns and make any necessary adjustments to your spending. To increase return on investment, reallocate resources to successful initiatives.

Use different budgets for different campaigns, ad groups, or keywords and see what works best. By experimenting with various funding levels, improvements and optimizations may be made.

Bidding Methods and Varieties:

Setting the maximum cost-per-click (CPC) bid for each keyword manually. Allows for fine-grained management of bids placed on particular keywords.

Target CPA, Target ROAS, Maximize Clicks, and Enhanced CPC are only few of Google's automated bidding tactics. Adjusting bids based on performance targets is the focus of these tactics, which employ machine learning.

Improve your PPC campaign's ROI using Enhanced Cost-Per-Click (ECPC), an algorithm that automatically optimizes your bids based on past performance. Bids can be raised for clicks that are more likely to result in a sale.

Set a goal CPA (Cost-Per-Acquisition), and Google's algorithm will automatically change bids to achieve that CPA.

Set a goal ROAS (Return on Ad Spend) to optimize bids and increase your ROI. Perfect for online shops who want to measure their advertising ROI.

Allows Google to maximize conversions within a specified budget by automatically adjusting bids.

Optimizes for the greatest possible number of clicks within the set spending limit. Great for drawing more people to your website.

Budgeting wisely and using strategic bidding can help marketers get the most out of their Google Ads campaigns, reducing wasteful expenditure and increasing returns. Sustaining success requires constant evaluation, analysis, and tweaking.

Using Cost-Per-Click (CPC) For Your Ads

Successful digital advertising campaign management requires an understanding of Cost-Per-Click (CPC) and the optimization of advertising expenditures. CPC, or cost per click, is a popular pricing scheme that bills businesses every time one of their ads is clicked.

Managing cost-per-click (CPC) correctly may have a major impact on the effectiveness and ROI of your advertising efforts. Here's a quick rundown:

First, there's the CPC, or "cost per click," which is how much it will set you back for a person to click on your ad. It is settled via auctions in which marketers submit bids indicating how much they are ready to pay per click. Ad quality, relevancy, bid amount, and competition are only few of the variables that might affect CPC.

Ad Relevance and Quality: Advertising networks like Google Ads analyze ad quality, relevancy, and predicted click-through rates (CTRs) in setting CPC. Ads that are both high quality and relevant tend to have a lower CPC. The amount of the advertiser's bid has a major impact on the cost-per-click. CPC tends to increase in tandem with bid size, while ad quality is also a factor.

Maximizing Return on Investment in CPC: Making a Practical Financial Plan: Set a spending limit that makes sense for your campaign goals and the money you expect to make each click.

Track Progress: The cost-per-click, click-through rate, and number of conversions should all be regularly tracked and analyzed. Spending can be optimized by adjusting bids and budgets in light of this information.

Methods to Reduce Cost-Per-Click

The cost-per-click (CPC) of your advertisements may be lowered if you take the time to create more relevant ads with engaging content and prominent calls to action.

You may reduce your cost-per-click by zeroing down on keywords with less competition, such as long-tail or specialty searches. Ads that are well-aligned with keywords, provide a nice user experience, and show previous success have a higher quality score, all of which contribute to a lower cost per click.

Choose a bid strategy from among maximization of clicks, a target cost per acquisition (CPA), or a target return on ad spend (ROAS) provided by your advertising platform. These methods provide support for controlling costs and maximizing returns in line with campaign objectives.

CPC and budget optimization requires striking a balance between bid management, ad quality, and relevancy. If you want to get the most out of your advertising dollar, you need to keep an eye on key performance indicators and make modifications depending on what you learn.

Chapter 7: Ad Performance and Optimization

Improving the efficiency of your advertisements requires a persistent cycle of monitoring results and making adjustments. Ad performance and its effect on marketing goals may be measured by tracking several KPIs such as click-through rate (CTR), conversion rate (CR), cost per click (CPC), return on ad spend (ROAS), and total conversion volume.

Creating variants of advertisements to try out different aspects like headlines, graphics, CTAs, or ad content through A/B testing helps determine which elements are most successful. Alignment between advertising and landing pages may be achieved by optimizing both for user experience and relevancy, which in turn increases conversions.

It is essential to monitor the success of individual campaigns and ad groups and change spending accordingly. Spending more on successful campaigns makes them even more effective.

To further refine and optimize the keyword list by suspending ineffective terms and adding new, relevant ones, it is helpful to analyze keyword performance and determine which keywords produce the most useful traffic.

Ad content and creatives should be constantly refined to increase engagement and relevancy. Finding out what works best with the audience requires testing out various messages, graphics, and calls to action.

Maximum exposure during high-converting periods is ensured by reviewing ad schedules and bidding modifications to correspond with peak user activity hours and changing bids based on performance data.

Targeting parameters and audience subsets must be fine-tuned based on results. Targeting efficiency may be improved by using audience information to zero in on high-performing segments while ignoring low-engagement groupings. Ad extensions (including site links, callouts, and structured snippets) and other elements enhance ad exposure and informational value.

Campaign optimization relies on constant data monitoring and incremental tweaking. Consistent improvements to campaigns and improved alignment with marketing goals may be achieved by periodic assessment and refinement of plans to react to shifting trends and audience habits.

Understanding A/B Testing and Experimentation

Using A/B testing and experimentation, marketers and digital advertisers may evaluate many factors and adjust their approaches and campaigns accordingly.

Split testing, commonly known as A/B testing, compares two variants of an advertisement, website, or other piece by showing one version (the control) to one group of people and the other (the variation) to another group. The objective is to find the variant that performs best in terms of click-through rates, conversions, and audience engagement. This technique allows for data-driven decisions to be made in order to boost the effectiveness of campaigns by providing measurable data and insights into customer behavior and preferences.

During experimentation, you'll zero in on what needs tweaking, speculate on what may change as a result, and then put your theories to the test. Elements to test might include ad language, graphics, layout and design, and timing or placement of advertising. Results from A/B testing may be used to make educated judgments and hone tactics, with the best tweaks being carried over to subsequent campaigns for continuous optimization.

Marketers may improve the success of their campaigns using A/B testing and other forms of experimentation. Constant testing and analysis allows firms to zero in on what works, make necessary adjustments, and boost the overall efficiency of their campaigns.

Keeping Track of Your Ad's Performance

Ad tracking and tweaking is a crucial part of any successful advertising effort. There are a number of essential procedures that must be taken to guarantee the efficacy of commercials and maximize the efficiency of marketing campaigns.

To begin, it is necessary to establish Key Performance Indicators (KPIs) that correspond to your advertising goals. Click-through rates (CTRs), conversion rates, cost-per-acquisition (CPAs), and return-on-ad-spending (ROASs) are all examples of metrics that might be used.

The next stage is to put monitoring systems in place. Ad performance may be tracked and monitored with the use of technologies like Google Analytics, Facebook Pixel, and platform-specific analytics.

These parameters must be monitored on a regular basis. This requires data analysis to determine which advertisements are successful and which are not. The ability to spot patterns and trends in the data is crucial for making sound judgments.

Using A/B testing is a smart move. You may learn what aspects of your ads (such as the language, images, CTAs, and audience targeting) are most effective through testing.

The importance of basing budget allocation on performance cannot be overstated. Spend more on successful commercials and less on unsuccessful ones, or at least give the unsuccessful ones some thought about getting a makeover.

Ad campaigns may be continuously optimized for improved outcomes through this iterative process of measuring ad performance, analyzing data, making modifications, and re-evaluating.

Chapter 8: Different Techniques for Remarketing

To begin, you can start with using pixels. You must first incorporate tags or pixels into your webpage. These nuggets of code make it possible to monitor site visitors' actions. Google Ads, Facebook, and LinkedIn are just a few of the widely used platforms that include pixel and tag choices to aid in efficient remarketing campaigns.

Divide your audience into subsets based on how they interact with your website. Make sure your advertisements are catered to each group by targeting their unique interests and behaviors. For instance, present product-focused advertising to people who saw certain things but didn't make a purchase, boosting the relevancy of your content.

Use dynamic remarketing advertisements, which update themselves to feature items and information in which people have expressed interest after visiting your site. By highlighting products users have shown interest in, this degree of customization greatly boosts conversion rates.

Remarketing that spans several ad networks and social media channels allows you to reach a wider audience. Re-engaging disinterested clients is more likely when you keep them interested across many channels.

Ad Frequency and Sequencing: Avoid ad fatigue by carefully managing the frequency of your remarketing advertisements. It's helpful to sequence ads so that they tell a story or offer context over several impressions.

Offer exclusive deals and incentives to bring back customers and get them to take the activities you want them to take. Exclusive offers may be incredibly successful in raising conversion rates among returning visitors.

Abandoned Cart Remarketing: Reach out to those who started an order but never finished it.

Incentives and gentle reminders about their abandoned things may encourage people to complete the transaction.

The length of time that has elapsed since a user's previous visit might inform your remarketing approach. Make sure your messages are tailored to the interests and actions of your users.

Optimization and Testing: Continuously optimize your remarketing efforts by experimenting with alternative ad formats, text, images, and calls to action. Methods can be honed with regular testing.

Privacy and Security Always follow applicable data protection laws and honor the users' right to privacy. To guarantee that your remarketing activities are in accordance with privacy rules and respect users' choices, be forthright about how data is used and allow consumers control over their preferences.

The success of your remarketing efforts, allowing you to re-engage potential consumers and increase conversion rates, may be greatly increased by implementing a mix of these tactics.

Setting the Perfect Remarketing Campaign

There are a few fundamental stages to creating effective remarketing campaigns. Before you start marketing to your site's users, you need to divide them into groups depending on their behavior while on your site. If you want to increase revenue, website traffic, or brand recognition, set some concrete objectives for your campaign.

Create engaging advertising material that stands out visually and is tailored to certain demographics. Try out several ad types, such as photos, videos, and carousel advertisements, to find what your audience responds to best. Use dynamic advertisements to display items and services that consumers have shown interest in. Ads should only link to relevant, user-friendly, and conversion-optimized landing sites.

Ad frequency should be carefully managed to prevent consumers from being overwhelmed, and testing different times may help identify peak response periods. Use a mix of Google Ads, social media, and email to reach your target audience in as many ways as possible. To find the most successful advertising strategies, use split testing to compare two groups' ads, messages, and audiences.

Mobile optimization is essential since mobile users now account for a sizable share of overall site visitors. Keep tabs on how things are going with your campaign and use analytics to hone down on what's working. Maintain protection of customer information and provide discounts to get customers back. The key to successful remarketing is to know your audience, provide them with relevant and unique material, and refine your approach based on data.

Cost Effective Remarketing Techniques

You may divide your target market into subgroups and tailor your message to each one using audience segmentation and personalization techniques. Make sure that your messaging and deals are unique for each group.

Dynamic remarketing involves serving advertising to users based on what they've shown interest in recently.

Ad frequency capping allows you to limit the number of times a person is exposed to your advertising.

Remarket to people across all of the devices they use while keeping your messaging consistent.

Customers that have previously converted should be excluded to reduce unnecessary advertising.

Finding new clients that are similar to your current ones is called a "lookalike audience," and it involves analyzing your customer database.

Remarket to those who started a purchase but didn't finish it using the "abandoned cart" tactic.

Sequencing and timing: Try out several scheduling options for your remarketing advertising to see what works best.

Content and Ad Creatives: Make ads that are interesting and relevant to users.

Continuous testing and tweaking of your campaigns will reveal which methods yield the best results.

Ad Placement: To maximize exposure, rotate your ads across many channels.

Tailor your strategy to the various phases of the customer's journey by providing them with appropriate material and incentives at the appropriate times.

Keeping in mind user privacy and preventing ad fatigue, implementing these tactics may greatly improve the efficiency of your remarketing operations. Improve your tactics by analyzing data and stats on a regular basis.

Remarketing Ads for Boosting ROI

First, learn who they are by dividing them into groups according to how they interact with your site or app. Learn the motivations of your customers so you may better target your adverts to them.

Make ads that appeal to certain groups of people by tailoring their message to them. Showcase the goods and services they've expressed interest in with dynamic content. Create brand-appropriate and enticing written and graphic content.

Use a variety of channels, including Google Ads, social media, and targeted networks, to maximize the effectiveness of your advertisements. Find the sweet spot between how often and when to show ads to prevent annoying people.

Make use of sophisticated methods of targeting, such as "lookalike" audiences and "behavioral" targeting. Users who are similar to your current consumers or who engage in comparable online activities might be targeted in this way.

Constantly analyze data, tweak ad content, and fine-tune targeting to increase return on investment and boost outcomes from your remarketing efforts.

Chapter 9: Boosting Your Brand Awareness

Improving a product's name recognition may be accomplished in a number of ways. The brand's beliefs and solutions may be better presented through consistent and compelling content development across several channels.

Relationship building and brand awareness may be achieved through social media by actively engaging with the audience through content sharing and participation in relevant topics.

Brand awareness may be greatly increased by forming partnerships with influential people or organizations in the target market. Brand awareness is strengthened when logos and other visual components are kept consistent throughout all promotional materials. Brand visibility may be improved by engaging in public relations initiatives that result in news coverage and by publicizing the brand's story or accomplishments. The success of these endeavors relies on their consistency.

Google Ads and Brand Awareness

Increasing your brand's exposure and familiarity across the Google network requires a deliberate and methodical approach using Google Ads.

One efficient technique is through Display Network Campaigns, which enable the placement of visually compelling adverts on multiple websites. These commercials, which frequently take the shape of images or other forms of rich media, are designed to attract a wide audience and establish the advertised brand's credibility.

Google's YouTube, a video-sharing website, also offers effective advertising options. Brand recognition may be greatly increased via the production of interesting and educational video content. To guarantee that you only pay for interested viewers, TrueView advertising let them skip after a few seconds.

Search Ads that use brand-related keywords can boost search engine rankings and increase brand awareness. With these advertising, you can manage the language used to describe your company whenever potential customers look for the goods and services you offer.

Display Remarketing in Google Ads allows you to go out to people who have engaged with your brand before but did not take any action. By targeting these users with advertising throughout the Google Display Network, you can get them to think of your company every time they see one of those ads.

Branding goals, rather than monetary ones, should be prioritized while developing out campaigns.

Brand awareness efforts may be better evaluated with the use of metrics like impressions, reach, and frequency.

Create ads with content and message that reflect your brand's values and appeal to your demographic. The success of these many advertising mediums depends on compelling and consistent messaging across all of them.

Compelling Ad Content for Boosting Brand Recognition

There are a few essentials for creating engaging advertising material that can help people remember your business. Start by developing a brand slogan that stands out from the crowd and articulates what makes your company special. Emphasize your company's unique selling points, such as high-quality products, excellent service, and cutting-edge ideas. Draw in your intended audience using eye-catching imagery, interesting narrative, and a consistent tone.

Put your brand's character into the ad so that customers may relate to it on an emotional level. Use emotions that are consistent with your brand's values, such as comedy, empathy, or inspiration. Make use of high-quality visual content that exemplifies your brand's ethos. Make sure the ad material seems like it belongs to your company by using the same colors, fonts, and images throughout.

Be sure to end your video with a strong CTA that compels viewers to learn more about your company. Direct the audience to the next logical step in the process, whether that's visiting your website, signing up for your newsletter, or completing a purchase. To increase consumer confidence in your product, you may share customer endorsements, testimonials, or success stories.

Last but not least, be consistent and persistent in your marketing efforts across all platforms. Consumers' memories of your brand will be strengthened by constant exposure to your brand's messaging. Increasing the likelihood of brand recognition and retention requires a unified brand voice and visual identity across all channels.

Target Audiences Reach and Engagement

Consider the following tactics to properly attract and captivate your intended audience:

Step one is to do some serious digging into the demographics, habits, hobbies, and pain points of your intended audience. Based on this information, we may create targeted marketing materials that speak directly to their interests.

Construct Intriguing Material Make material that is useful and interesting to your target audience. Blog articles, videos, infographics, and podcasts are all good examples of this kind of material that may be tailored to the mediums on which your target audience is most likely to be found.

Engage with your target audience via social media platforms. Content should be adapted for each platform, as audiences there have different demographics and online habits.

Personalize Communication: Employ personalization in your communication tactics, calling your audience by their names, giving tailored suggestions, and adapting your messaging to their interests. Adding a personal touch increases participation and strengthens the bond with the audience.

Use search engine optimization and paid advertising to raise your visibility and attract more of your ideal customers. Maximize your exposure and bring in organic visitors by using keywords associated with what they're looking for. Also, think about using sponsored search advertising to zero in on your desired demographic.

Engage in conversation on both ends and learn from the experience. Start debates, interact with your audience, and pay close attention to their comments and suggestions. Creating a group of dedicated followers requires establishing rapport with them and demonstrating that you respect their input.

Partner and collaborate with those who already have your target audience's attention, such as influencers, other companies, or industry experts. By forming strategic alliances, you may increase your visibility and authority in your field.

Always evaluate how your strategies are faring and make adjustments as necessary. Analytical tools can help you determine whether strategies are successful. Constantly fine-tune your methods of engagement by adjusting to new facts.

You may successfully contact and engage your target audience, resulting in better relationships and more brand success, by following these methods and maintaining a dynamic strategy that is responsive to changes in audience behavior and preferences.

Chapter 10: SEO and Google Ads

Using SEO knowledge to improve your Google Ads campaigns is a must. If you use Google advertising, you may get keyword data in the form of search query reports, which can provide you with essential insights into the actual search keywords that trigger your advertising.

You may use this information to better target your ads, but it can also help direct your organic SEO approach by illuminating popular search terms and user preferences.

Keyword performance analysis in Google Ads is another way to learn which terms are most responsible for bringing in customers. In order to boost organic search ranks and relevancy, this information may be utilized to enhance website content in accordance with these high-converting keywords.

Google Ads' A/B testing functionality provides concrete data on which ad variations perform better with a certain target population. You can use this information to make your paid advertisements and organic search results more in sync with one another by tweaking your meta descriptions, title tags, and website content.

Additionally, concentrating on matching landing page content with ad messaging not only enhances Quality Score in Google Ads but also adds to greater organic search ranks. By harmonizing these elements, you can improve the quality of both your paid and organic traffic, as well as provide a more consistent and enjoyable user experience.

Boosting Ad Performance with SEO

Combining paid advertising with organic search optimization methods is the key to integrating SEO tactics into Google Ads. It is crucial to optimize landing pages for both organic search and ad relevance and to match ad content with high-performing keywords. Businesses may increase their ad quality scores and click-through rates by doing keyword research to uncover high-performing keywords and then using those keywords wisely in their ad text and landing sites. Ad extensions like sitelinks and structured snippets that are consistent with the website's SEO strategy also help boost ad exposure and user engagement.

If you want your ads to perform better, you can use SEO to your advantage by adapting them based on what you learn from your organic search efforts. Advertisers may improve the efficiency of their Google Ads campaigns by examining the success of organic keywords, click-through rates, and user behavior. Ads will have their content optimized so that they mirror the most popular organic strategies and user tastes. Aligning ad landing pages with highly rated organic pages on the site not only enforces brand consistency but also enhances the user experience, potentially affecting ad effectiveness by lowering bounce rates and increasing conversions. In summary, maximizing the effectiveness of both paid and organic search requires a coordinated and well-thought-out strategy, which can be achieved by integrating SEO knowledge with Google Ads tactics.

Ads Optimization for Increased Search Engine Visibility

Ads that perform well in search engines are the result of careful consideration of several elements. It's vital to write ads in line with relevant keywords and the goal of the searcher. Ad headlines, descriptions, and display URLs should all make organic use of effective keywords. The use of ad extensions, such as site links and callout extensions, increases the exposure of ads and gives prospective consumers with more information. In addition, search engine visibility and user experience are significantly improved by optimizing landing pages to ensure they are closely matched with ad content, are responsive, load quickly, and offer relevant, keyword-rich material.

Better ad placement may be achieved with a deeper understanding of SEO and its nuances. Ad rank may be improved with the help of an in-depth understanding of what goes into determining organic search rank, including things like keyword relevancy, website authority, and user experience. Marketers may improve ad targeting, copywriting, and landing page performance by learning from SEO best practices. Ad quality and relevance are both increased as a result of this alignment, and the overall ranking of ads is also strengthened. Furthermore, regularly monitoring SEO trends and algorithms helps advertisers to change their ad campaigns efficiently, ensuring they stay in sync with the developing dynamics of search engine ranking, thereby maximizing ad performance and exposure. When search engine optimization (SEO) concepts are used to ad optimization strategies, a synergistic effect is created that boosts both the advertisements' ranks and their exposure in SERPs.

Chapter 11: Instant Results and Boosting Visibility

There are various strategies you may employ in Google Ads to create fast results and boost your brand's online visibility.

Begin with well-planned Search Engine Marketing (SEM) campaigns that make use of specific keywords and organized advertising. When people look for items or services linked to your brand, your advertising will appear at the top of the search engine results page.

Make use of PPC advertising, in which you will only be charged for clicks. This method is not only excellent in generating traffic and sales, but it also has a low cost of entry.

Ad extensions should be a part of every Google Ads strategy. Ad exposure is boosted and viewers are given additional information about your business and products thanks to ad extensions including site links, callouts, and geographical details.

Take use of Geo-Targeting tools to focus on certain regions. With this method, you may reach out to potential clients in the right places, increasing your brand's exposure to a more niche demographic.

You may increase the visibility and reach of your Google Ads campaign by using clever bid tactics. By targeting the correct audience at the right time, smart bidding tactics can boost both the exposure and effectiveness of your adverts.

Techniques that Generates Instant Results

A laser-like concentration on producing instant results is essential when implementing quick results methods in Google Ads. Identifying high-potential, relevant keywords for your advertisements begins with doing keyword research. Long-tail keywords with demonstrable purpose should be prioritized since they often result in more relevant clicks and greater conversion rates. Ensure these keywords correspond with your advertising aims and target audience.

Make sure your ad wording is very pertinent to the keywords you've chosen. Create ads that are interesting to potential customers by highlighting the benefits they will receive from purchasing your goods or services. Create compelling CTAs that encourage users to take action, whether that's completing a purchase, joining up, or inquiring for more details.

Ad extensions allow you to add more information to your ads and increase their visibility. Structured snippets, callouts, and site links are all examples of extensions that provide more information about your products and services and so increase the possibility of clicks. Optimize your landing pages for conversions and quick load times by making sure they are consistent with the content of your ads.

Whether you're aiming to boost website traffic, revenue, leads, or brand awareness, make sure your campaign's objectives are crystal clear and quantifiable. Keep a careful eye on your advertising' success by tracking and analyzing data like CTR, Conversion Rate, and ROAS. Make changes to your bids, budget, and ad schedule based on which advertisements and keywords are producing the greatest results.

To get back in touch with visitors who explored your site before but didn't make a purchase, retargeting campaigns are worth considering. The goal of this tactic is to get clients who shown interest back to your business. Additionally, experiment with multiple ad forms, such as responsive search advertising, display advertisements, or video ads, to identify which formats resonate most with your audience.

Ad components like as headlines, descriptions, and pictures should be regularly A/B tested to ensure optimal performance. Optimize depending on the results to optimize ad performance. Finally, to take advantage of fresh prospects for rapid wins, you should keep up with the latest trends and features in Google Ads. Keep in mind that techniques aimed at producing rapid outcomes require constant monitoring and adjustment to ensure long-term viability.

Approaches to Boost Visibility Using Click-Through Rates

Improving your content's exposure and the number of people who choose to click on it calls for a multifaceted approach to marketing. Here are several tried and true methods:

Focus on Search Engine Optimization (SEO) to raise your site's rankings in relevant search results. To do this, you must use appropriate keywords, provide high-quality content, tweak your meta descriptions, titles, and headers, and check that your site is technically solid. If you want more people to see your site, you should optimize it so that it ranks better in search engine results.

Make Useful Titles and Meta Descriptions: Write catchy titles and meta descriptions to draw readers in. These items typically appear at the top of users' search page results. Click-through rates may be dramatically increased with a more captivating title and description that do justice to the content.

High-Quality material Generation: Create material that is both educational and interesting, and which responds to the wants and needs of your intended audience. This material could be written posts, video segments, infographics, or audio recordings.

When consumers find something of interest, they are more likely to click around your site.

Using Structured Data and Rich Snippets can improve your website's visibility in search engine results. These snippets add value to search engine results by providing visitors with supplementary information right where they are.

With the proliferation of mobile devices, it's more important than ever to give attention to making your website mobile-friendly. Click-through rates may be increased by providing a better user experience, which is achieved through a combination of a mobile-friendly layout and quick page loads.

Utilize appealing Visuals: Incorporate appealing and relevant visuals, such as photographs, videos, infographics, and charts, to make your material more engaging. Users are typically enticed to click for further information by eye-catching design features.

Constantly test variations of your content's headlines, pictures, calls to action, and layout using A/B testing and optimization tools. The greatest way to improve your content's click-through rates is to find out what your audience responds to best, and A/B testing can help you do just that.

Use compelling and understandable calls to action (CTAs) to direct users toward the desired outcomes. An effective call to action (CTA) may boost conversions by encouraging people to explore your content further.

When used together, these strategies may boost your content's discoverability and engagement rates, bringing in more readers and encouraging them to take action. Maintaining and enhancing these rates over time requires constant monitoring and modifications based on performance data.

Google Ads that Drives Instant Conversions

Rapid conversions are possible with the use of quick advertising methods. These methods are implemented in an effort to quickly acquire and convert prospective clients. Some strategies to think about are as follows.

Making Things Scarce and Time-RestrictedUrgency motivates people to take action. Promoting urgency in your advertising by using timers, stock warnings, or other time-sensitive information will help you close sales faster. Limiting supplies or reserving a special discount for the first 50 buyers are examples of scarcity strategies that instill a feeling of urgency and competition.

A compelling motivation to do action: Make sure your advertising include appealing call-to-actions that tell people what to do. A compelling CTA, such as "Shop Now," "Sign Up Today," or "Limited Time Offer - Act Now," urges customers to act quickly.

Advertising incentives such as price reductions, free trials, and other limited-time offers may significantly increase the number of people who make a purchase after seeing your ad. Users who are looking for a deal will be drawn to your ad if you prominently feature these incentives and push them to take immediate action.

It is essential to have a landing page that is optimized for conversions and flows naturally from the ad content. Make sure the landing page conveys the intended message of the ad and simplifies the user's path to conversion.

Since mobile devices now account for a sizable share of all internet traffic, it's crucial that your advertising techniques cater to this growing demographic. By improving the user experience, mobile-optimized advertisements and landing pages increase conversion rates.

Use retargeting advertisements to get in touch with people who have shown interest in your brand in the past. Those users are more likely to make a quick decision if the advertising they see contain personalized messaging or incentives.

By combining urgency, clear CTAs, compelling promos, optimized landing pages, mobile compatibility, and retargeting, these quick ad techniques may effectively drive conversions, pushing visitors to take rapid and decisive action. To ensure these tactics have the greatest possible impact and can be maintained over time, regular analysis and optimization are required.

Performance Assessment for Timely Results

When time is of the essence, it is essential to use well-defined KPIs to evaluate progress. Click-through rates (CTRs) in digital marketing provide a quick read on how interesting users find your content or ad. The higher your CTR, the more engaged your audience appears to be with your content and the more likely they are to take the next step and click on an ad or a link. The conversion rate is the proportion of visitors who do the intended action, such as buying something or signing up for a service. If your conversion rate increases significantly, then your campaigns or content are successfully eliciting the intended responses.

And your landing pages' and content's relevancy and engagement can be quickly gauged by looking at the bounce rate, which is the percentage of visitors that leave your site after reading only one page. A reduced bounce rate frequently suggests that the content corresponds well with what consumers are seeking, hence potentially leading to increased conversions. Another crucial indicator is return on investment (ROI), which measures the financial gain made in comparison to the initial outlay. If your marketing activities are successful in producing income quickly, then your return on investment (ROI) will be positive.

Furthermore, engagement rates provide instantaneous feedback on the interest and participation of your content's audience through social media marketing tools like likes, shares, and comments. If your audience is actively participating with your content, you can expect to see rapid growth in both audience size and brand recognition. To achieve long-term success for your firm, it is essential to connect these indicators with your overall goals and long-term strategy.

Printed in Great Britain
by Amazon